GRAPHIC LIBRARY®

CARTOON★NATION
EST. presents 1776
THE U.S. CONSTITUTION

by Christine Peterson
illustrated by Brian Bascle

CONSULTANT:
Philip Bigler, Director
The James Madison Center
James Madison University
Harrisonburg, Virginia

Capstone press®
Mankato, Minnesota

Graphic Library is published by Capstone Press,
151 Good Counsel Drive, P.O. Box 669, Mankato, Minnesota 56002.
www.capstonepress.com

Copyright © 2009 by Capstone Press, a Capstone Publishers company. All rights reserved.
No part of this publication may be reproduced in whole or in part, or stored in a
retrieval system, or transmitted in any form or by any means, electronic, mechanical,
photocopying, recording, or otherwise, without written permission of the publisher.
For information regarding permission, write to Capstone Press, 151 Good Counsel Drive,
P.O. Box 669, Dept. R, Mankato, Minnesota 56002.
Printed in the United States of America

1 2 3 4 5 6 13 12 11 10 09 08

Library of Congress Cataloging-in-Publication Data
Peterson, Christine, 1961–
    The U.S. Constitution / by Christine Peterson; illustrated by Brian Bascle.
    p. cm. — (Graphic library. Cartoon nation)
    Summary: "In cartoon format, explains how the U.S. Constitution was created, how it
has been amended, and why it is still important today" — Provided by publisher.
    Includes bibliographical references and index.
    ISBN-13: 978-1-4296-1984-4 (hardcover)
    ISBN-10: 1-4296-1984-8 (hardcover)
    ISBN-13: 978-1-4296-2856-3 (softcover pbk.)
    ISBN-10: 1-4296-2856-1 (softcover pbk.)
    1. United States. Constitution — Juvenile literature. 2. United States — Politics and
government — 1775–1783 — Juvenile literature. 3. United States — Politics and government
— 1783–1789 — Juvenile literature. 4. Constitutional history — United States — Juvenile
literature. I. Bascle, Brian, ill. II. Title. III. Series.
E303.P47 2009
342.7302'9 — dc22   2008000487

Art Director and Designer
Bob Lentz

Production Designer
Kim Brown

Cover Artist
Kelly Brown

Editor
Christopher L. Harbo

TABLE OF CONTENTS

Long before electric lights and indoor plumbing, a group of 55 farmers, lawyers, and former soldiers met to form a new government. Their ideas were revolutionary and untested. But the government created by the U.S. Constitution proved to be a major hit.

The Constitution describes the role of the national government and limits its powers. For more than 220 years, the Constitution has guided leaders through wars and political change. It has caused citizens to fight for equal rights. It has withstood years of change and challenges.

The country has sure changed since the last time we were here.

Yes, but I can still see where I carved my initials on this chair.

When the Founding Fathers created the U.S. Constitution, they wanted citizens to have a say in their government. That's why the U.S. government has three branches. And though the Constitution has been amended, the principles of government it spells out have remained basically unchanged.

We may have come up with the Constitution, but it's the people who make it work.

Founding Father — one of a handful of men who were important in helping the colonies become one country

NEW COUNTRY, OLD GOVERNMENT

The American people didn't always have a voice in their government. Hundreds of years ago, America got its start as a group of 13 colonies ruled by Great Britain. Colonists came to America in hope of more personal freedoms and a better life. But Britain's rule and taxes followed them to America.

The colonists were governed by British laws, but they had no voice in the government. Instead, they were forced to obey a long list of laws and pay high taxes. And who could they thank? That's right — Britain's King George III.

These new taxes and a lack of freedom angered colonists. They protested new laws and taxes on paper products and tea. In 1773, colonists dumped crates of tea into Boston Harbor. War was brewing in the colonies.

In 1775, war broke out between the colonies and Great Britain. Leaders knew that to win the war, the colonies must work together. The 13 colonies formed a government to unite them during the war. Most states referred to the Articles of Confederation as a league of friendship. The Articles weren't strong, but they were enough to bind the colonies together during the war.

After eight long years of war, the colonies won their independence from Great Britain in 1783.

HEROES OR TRAITORS?

Thomas Jefferson, Benjamin Franklin, and George Washington were America's first heroes. Yet in 1776, they were all considered traitors and criminals by the British. In fact, all 56 men who signed the Declaration of Independence were considered criminals by King George III.

The Founding Fathers didn't have long to celebrate the nation's victory. Trouble now cropped up in the states. The Articles of Confederation were too weak to be a lasting form of government. Under the Articles, states were still more powerful than the national government. States could make laws, pass taxes, and even choose their own form of money.

But most of the states had one thing in common. They were in debt from the Revolutionary War. State governments forced farmers and landowners to pay heavy taxes. Anyone who couldn't pay their bill was put in jail. Plus, their land was taken by the state government.

Daniel Shays was a Massachusetts farmer and former soldier. He had lost much of his land. Shays was now broke and angry. In 1786, he organized a group of farmers to fight against unfair laws passed by the states.

Soon, the United States was on the brink of total collapse. In Massachusetts, farmers fought local militia in several battles. Leaders from the states agreed it was time to take action.

WEAK GOVERNMENT

After winning the Revolutionary War, the United States had won its independence. But the new government was weak. States had the real power. States passed their own laws. Each state had its own money. States could call out their own militias but could refuse to defend the nation, even if asked by the national government.

In May 1787, delegates from 12 states gathered in Philadelphia to strengthen the national government. It wasn't an easy task.

It's time we got this government in shape.

delegate — a person who represents other people at a convention

Some delegates favored keeping the Articles of Confederation. Others believed that a new national government was the way to go. Future president James Madison was a fortune-teller of sorts. He knew that a weak national government meant doom for the new nation. Madison and fellow Virginian Edmund Randolph came up with the Virginia Plan.

Under Madison's Virginia Plan, the new government would divide its powers and duties between three branches. The government's legislative branch would also have two parts, called a House and Senate. But no one branch would be more powerful than another.

I see a strong national government in this country's future, Mr. Randolph.

I could have told you that without a crystal ball.

Madison the Magnificent

But delegates were divided over the number of state representatives in the new government. Large states wanted the number of representatives based on population. Delegates from small states cried "foul." They feared that large states would control the government.

Delegates finally struck a deal, called the Great Compromise. It gave states an equal number of representatives in the Senate. In the House, the number of representatives would be based on a state's population.

After much debate and compromise, delegates finally embraced Madison's plan for a new government. Delegates agreed that an elected president would lead the executive branch of government. The legislative branch would make laws for the country. The judicial branch would make sure that new laws followed the Constitution.

A New Government at Last

With most of the major issues ironed out, delegates finally approved the new Constitution. Leaders in the 13 states would soon vote on the new government. Approval would be a slam dunk, right?

Not so fast. Some delegates felt the new government took too many rights away from states. Others thought the new government didn't protect individual freedoms.

Two main groups debated the pros and cons of the Constitution. Federalists believed the Constitution provided for a strong government. James Madison, Alexander Hamilton, and John Jay wrote letters in support of the Constitution. Newspapers published these letters, which became known as the Federalist Papers.

Anti-Federalists believed the Constitution gave too much power to the federal government. They wanted personal rights and freedoms guaranteed in writing. Some Anti-Federalists even refused to show up at state conventions to approve the Constitution. They hoped there wouldn't be enough delegates to vote on the Constitution.

But Federalists weren't playing games. Some Feds forced Anti-Feds to attend state conventions. One by one, the states voted. Delaware was the first state to approve the new government on December 7, 1787. Soon, Pennsylvania, New Jersey, Georgia, and Connecticut all passed the Constitution.

The new government was picking up steam. On June 21, 1788, New Hampshire became the ninth state to pass the new government. The Constitution was now the official law of the land.

After the document was approved, many states believed the Constitution still needed to protect the basic rights of citizens. One famous citizen agreed. In April 1789, George Washington became the first president of the United States. In his first speech as president, Washington asked Congress to consider amending the Constitution to protect personal freedoms.

You only need to make a few changes. The document is still pretty solid.

Leading Federalist James Madison soon changed his own mind. Madison came to believe that if the new government was to succeed, a Bill of Rights had to be added to the Constitution.

If we're going to win this round, we'll have to make some changes.

Once again, Madison began writing. He came up with 17 amendments, which he presented to Congress. Congress narrowed them down to 12 and sent the list to the states for approval. The states passed 10 of the amendments, creating a Bill of Rights.

amendment — a change made to a law or a legal document

What are these rights? The Bill of Rights guarantees U.S. citizens the right to say what they believe and get their news from a free press.

Citizens like you can attend the church of your choice. You may also gather to protest something you don't like.

Under the Bill of Rights, citizens can own guns. They also don't have to worry about surprise searches of their homes by the government. And if you are charged with a crime, you have a right to a jury trial. If that jury finds you innocent, you can't be tried for that crime again.

FATHER-OF-THE-CONSTITUTION

For such a little guy, James Madison left a large legacy as the Father of the Constitution. Madison, a Virginia planter, was actually a quiet man. He spent hours before the Constitutional Convention researching other forms of government. Some say he actually arrived in Philadelphia with a plan in place for the new federal government.

The Founding Fathers didn't want their new government led by another king. That's why they decided a president would lead the executive branch.

No more kings for us.

GEORGE WASHINGTON

But the Founding Fathers wrote rules in the Constitution so presidents don't become too powerful. To become president, individuals must have been born in the United States. They must be at least 35 years old and have lived in the country for the past 14 years. Under the Constitution, presidents serve four-year terms. Today, presidents can only be elected to two terms, thanks to the 22nd Amendment.

JOHN F. KENNEDY

Hey, Ike. Is it my turn yet?

DWIGHT D. EISENHOWER

Not so fast, Kennedy. I've got a few years left in my term.

U.S. presidents wear many hats. They are the commander-in-chief of the U.S. military. As the nation's head of state, they meet with leaders from other countries. Presidents are in charge of the federal government and serve as boss to thousands of employees.

WASHINGTON

LINCOLN

ROOSEVELT

But presidents can't do everything they want. Sometimes they need to get approval from Congress. For example, presidents can appoint justices to serve on the Supreme Court and make treaties with other nations. But presidents must win the Senate's approval before these appointments or treaties become final.

That's a mighty long list. You'll have to wait for our approval.

CONGRESS

PRESIDENTIAL ELECTIONS

ELECTOR

ELECTOR

And the winner and new U.S. president is . . .

When voting for president, U.S. citizens are really choosing a group of electors. This group makes up the nation's Electoral College. This college isn't a school. It's a group of people who cast the final votes for president.

You know that the Constitution provides the framework for the nation's government, but how do laws get made? This job was given to the elected members of the legislative branch.

In the legislative branch, the House of Representatives and Senate make up the U.S. Congress. Remember the Great Compromise? That deal continues today. Each state elects two senators to serve in the Senate. The number of members from each state in the House of Representatives is based on population. Since 1911, the number of representatives has been set at 435.

QUICK-FACT

Currently, California has the most representatives with 53. Seven states have just one representative in the House.

The main duty of Congress is to pass new laws for the country. Laws can get their start as an idea from a member of Congress, the president, or citizens like you.

An idea for a law is introduced in Congress as a bill. House or Senate committees review the bill to decide if it would make a strong law. Committee members can reject the bill or send it to the House and Senate for debate and a vote. If Congress approves the bill, it goes to the president for signing.

The Constitution gives presidents the right to **veto**, or reject, any bill they don't believe will benefit the nation. Congress can override a veto if two-thirds of its members vote in favor of the vetoed bill.

Veto or law. Veto or law. What should I do?

Ahhh come on, fella. Make up your mind.

veto — the power or right to stop a bill from becoming law

To be fair and balanced, the national government needs a branch to make sure that all new laws follow the Constitution. That's just one of the many jobs of the judicial branch.

Referred to as the highest court in the land, the Supreme Court hears cases on the meaning of laws. Justices examine how the laws are applied and whether they are in keeping with the Constitution.

Each year, the Supreme Court is asked to hear hundreds of cases. But they only choose a select few to review. When deciding a case, justices listen to both sides of the case and review any laws that may apply. Then the court issues a decision in the case. Win or lose, the Supreme Court's decision is final.

How are we ever going to choose a case?

Nine justices make up the Supreme Court. Justices can serve on the court for life or until they choose to retire or resign. Justices can be impeached and, if convicted, removed from office. But this has never happened.

THE SUPREMES

Supreme Court justices have all been lawyers. Some have served as governors or members of the president's Cabinet. One justice, William Howard Taft, was a former president.

The chief justice leads the Supreme Court and the judicial branch and has special duties that come with the job. As head of the Court, the chief justice presides over any impeachment trials in the Senate. This leader also gives the oath of office to newly elected presidents.

Repeat after me, Mr. President.

Repeat after me, Mr. President.

Back in 1787, the Founding Fathers had a good vision for the United States.

But they couldn't predict everything. They knew the Constitution would sometimes have to be changed.

First came the Bill of Rights, but the changes didn't stop there. Since 1791, the Constitution has been amended 17 more times. But all these changes don't mean that the original document was weak. Instead, these changes show how the document can be adapted to meet the needs of a growing and changing country.

But changing the Constitution isn't easy. Most amendments start in Congress. First, an amendment must be introduced into Congress. Then, two-thirds of both the House of Representatives and Senate must vote to propose an amendment.

If passed by Congress, the amendment moves on to the states for approval. To become law, three-fourths of all state legislatures must approve the amendment.

CONSTITUTIONAL AMENDMENTS

Thousands of amendments have been proposed, but the Constitution has only 27 amendments today. Here are some major amendments that won approval:

The 13th Amendment made slavery illegal in the United States.

The 15th Amendment gave black men voting rights.

The 19th Amendment gave women the right to vote.

The 22nd Amendment limited a president to two terms in office. Each term lasts four years.

People from across the country and from around the world can visit the actual Constitution in the National Archives in Washington, D.C. Light and heat sensors help preserve the document while on display. Bulletproof glass covers the cases.

Each day, visitors can view all four pages of the original document. On Constitution Day, the Constitution is placed in a special case in the center of the rotunda at the National Archives. But what happens at night?

Ahh. I'd be happy to explain that. But first, we need a little electricity.

Each night, the Constitution is lowered into a vault. Once it's safe inside, heavy slabs of metal and concrete cover the vault.

But no ordinary vault will do for our Constitution. This vault can withstand fires, earthquakes, and even bomb blasts.

At night, you crawl into a warm bed. The same is true for our Constitution. Only its bed lies 20 feet below ground.

Hold on tight. We're going down.

Each morning, the Constitution automatically rises back to its case. It's ready and waiting for more visitors, like you.

25

Some nations have tried to copy the Constitution. Others have criticized it. But with each new challenge, the Constitution emerges stronger than ever. The basic government with three branches and a system of checks and balances still serves the people today.

Today, the basic ideas of the U.S. Constitution remain the same. Because of the Constitution, you have a say in government and the right to speak your mind in public.

You can elect leaders to represent you in government. And if those leaders don't do a good job, you can elect new ones to take their place. You could even be elected to serve in Congress or as president someday.

The Constitution has survived many challenges during our nation's history. But these tests have only made it stronger. The Constitution has changed to meet the needs of a growing nation.

The government created during that hot summer of 1787 remains a powerful symbol of freedom and democracy. The Founding Fathers held tight to their extraordinary ideas. They molded 13 states into a united nation that not even the Civil War could separate. The Constitution still represents the ideas they set forth so long ago.

CONSTITUTION DAY

Constitution Day is celebrated each year on September 17. This holiday honors the delegates who signed the historic document that day in 1787. In schools across the country, students like you read from the Constitution and learn about its history.

Time Line

July 4, 1776 — Delegates at the Second Continental Congress sign the Declaration of Independence, proclaiming the colonies' freedom from Great Britain.

November 15, 1777 — Congress approves the Articles of Confederation, creating a government to unite the states during war with Britain.

July 4, 1776

November 15, 1777

September 25, 1789 — Congress proposes 12 amendments to the Constitution. The states approve 10 amendments, creating the Bill of Rights in 1791.

December 6, 1865 — The 13th Amendment wins approval and outlaws slavery in the United States.

September 25, 1789

August 18, 1920 — Women finally win the right to vote when the 19th Amendment is passed by the states.

December 6, 1865

August 18, 1920

May 1787 — Delegates meet in Philadelphia for a constitutional convention to strengthen the U.S. government.

MAY 1787

September 17, 1787 — Delegates sign the Constitution at the Philadelphia State House in Philadelphia.

SEPTEMBER 17, 1787

June 21, 1788 — New Hampshire becomes the ninth state to approve the U.S. Constitution, and the new government becomes law.

JUNE 21, 1788

December 13, 1952 — The U.S. Constitution and Declaration of Independence move to the National Archives. Armed military troops and tanks guard the documents as they travel to the Archives.

DECEMBER 13, 1952

May 2005 — U.S. leaders create Constitution Day, a national holiday honoring the U.S. Constitution.

MAY 2005

GLOSSARY

amendment (uh-MEND-muhnt) — a change made to a law or a legal document

Articles of Confederation (AR-ti-kuhls UHV kuhn-fed-er-AY-shun) — the original set of laws governing the 13 American colonies during the Revolutionary War

Bill of Rights (BIL UHV RITES) — a list of 10 amendments to the Constitution that protect your right to speak freely, to practice religion, and other important rights

branch (BRANCH) — one of three parts of U.S. government

Cabinet (KA-buh-nit) — a group of advisers chosen by the president

delegate (DEL-uh-guht) — a person chosen to speak and act for others

democracy (di-MAH-kruh-see) — a form of government in which people can choose their leaders

Electoral College (ee-lehk-TOHR-uhl KAH-luhj) — the group of people that elects the president and vice president after the general election

Founding Father (FOUN-ding FAH-thur) — one of a handful of men who were important in helping the colonies become one country

impeach (im-PEECH) — to bring formal charges against a public official who may have committed a crime while in office

veto (VEE-toh) — the power or right to stop a bill from becoming law

READ MORE

Burgan, Michael. *The Creation of the U.S. Constitution*. Graphic History. Mankato, Minn.: Capstone Press, 2007.

Conway, John Richard. *A Look at the Constitution: Creating a More Perfect Union*. The Constitution of the United States. Berkeley Heights, N.J.: MyReportLinks.com Books, 2008.

Fradin, Dennis B. *The U.S. Constitution*. Turning Points in U.S. History. New York: Marshall Cavendish Benchmark, 2007.

O'Donnell, Liam. *Democracy*. Cartoon Nation. Mankato, Minn.: Capstone Press, 2008.

Price, Sean. *Designing America: The Constitutional Convention*. American History through Primary Sources. Chicago: Raintree, 2008.

INTERNET SITES

FactHound offers a safe, fun way to find Internet sites related to this book. All of the sites on FactHound have been researched by our staff.

Here's how:
1. Visit *www.facthound.com*
2. Choose your grade level.
3. Type in this book ID 1429619848 for age-appropriate sites. You may also browse subjects by clicking on letters, or by clicking on pictures and words.
4. Click on the Fetch It button.

FactHound will fetch the best sites for you!

INDEX

321.8 O   ICCRX   Circ 0 8/10
O'Donnell, Liam,
Democracy /

CENTRAL LIBRARY
05/10